Outside - In
Musing on life
As an
Autistic Poet

Alain English

Published by William Cornelius Harris UK

In collaboration

with

Second Chance

Supporting Mental Health in Performing Arts

ISBN 978- 1 - 291 - 99521 - 3

Copyright © Alain English 2014
All rights reserved

c/o Open Door, 224 Jamaica Road, London SE16

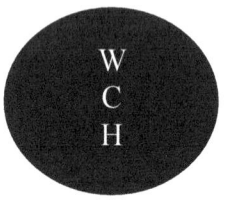

Second Chance

You may need it next

Contents

	Page	
Introduction		4
Weekender		5
The People We Don't See		7
The Sleeper on the Stair		8
Vallance Road		10
Depression is a most Unwelcome Guest		11
Losing My Mind on the Internet		12
I Am a Sex and Love Addict		13
Conversations are like Tennis Matches		14
Intimacy		15
The Dating Game		17
When Polly met Darren		19
Break up		20
Karma Complex		22
Learning Disability		24
The Ballad of Jack McGee		26
Love Is		33
Falling Forward		37
This Is Who I Am		41

Hi folks,

Thanks for picking up my first poetry collection. I penned these pieces to give a picture of what it's like living in a great city like London with an autistic learning disability and the way this affects your perceptions and relationships.

I hope you find the poems interesting and insightful.

Regards,

Alain English

Weekender

The weekend is here and these miserable evenings
Will see the chaotic predictable pleasures
Of many engaged in their chatter and drinking
The poison that powers the games they are playing
In pubs, on the streets, all the courting and fighting

That happens between all the regular people.
It stings me whenever I see all the people
I'm scared to approach and enduring these evenings
Alone and depressed, I'm afraid and I'm fighting
My fears by resisting my need for these pleasures,

By hiding myself in my room and I'm playing
Computer games, watching the telly, not drinking.
Detached from the buzz of the booze they are drinking
In town on a Saturday night when the people

Will flirt with themselves and each others, they're playing
A sexual game that enlivens their evenings
With many exciting adventures and pleasures.
How often does banter descend into fighting,
The petty stupidity triggers the fighting,

Emotions inflamed by the spirits they're drinking,
Immersing themselves in their chemical pleasures
Forgetting about how they're living as people

The days are so tiring with work and the evenings
Are spent in the pub with the footballers playing
On telly and others are gambling and playing
With money - they're hustling and others are fighting

Their friends or their partners and blighting their evenings
With anger brought forth in a torrent of drinking,
The swirling delirium drowning the people
In tedious ecstasy, dizzying pleasures,
The music that's always surrounding their pleasures

With rhythm, it's narrative constantly playing,
It speaks of the hopes and the fears of the people
Who live in the city, surviving and fighting,
Escaping reality dancing and drinking,
Enjoying the highs and the lows of their pleasures.
I'm all on my own in the evenings, aloof from the people,

No drinking, no fighting, no playing, no pleasures.

The People We Don't See

The poor and homeless on the street
They ask us for a little change
But we pretend they don't exist
For that's the way the city thinks
We see the beggars on the street

I wonder why I want to give
To them - their plight fills me with guilt
We see them when we're on the town
They ask us for a little change
With paper cups and cardboard signs

The faces hardened from the cold
And covered up in scars and mud
But we pretend they don't exist
They could be taking us for mugs

We don't think they deserve our cash
We're looking out for number one
For that's the way the city thinks
Absorbed within our petty lives
We never stop to think about
The people whom we never see
The poor and homeless on the street

The Sleeper on the Stair

"Hey there, you! Why did you call the police?" I looked up the stairwell, catching his reflection in the landing window. He was sitting there, same as before, unlit cigarette in his hand. I winced slightly. I didn't think he would come back, but he's there. I put my keys in my pocket and went up to see him.

The roof landing in my council block is a target for rough sleepers. The secure door on the ground floor is meant to keep out unwanted intruders but they still sneak in, especially during the winter months. But this was summer, and the man I saw above me had been there for several months.

I didn't call the police, not at first. I felt inclined to sympathise. I have been close to being homeless myself until I found the place where I live now. I found it only with the help of friends and contacts. In London, these are precious and can be hard to come by.

Aware of this, of how my situation was easier than his, I had tried to talk to him. I wanted to see if I could help him. It became apparent, through lack of will or know-how that I couldn't. I called in homeless outreach teams, but every time they turned up, he wasn't there.

So I tried to get rid of him myself, gently, by moving his cardboard bedding and disposing of it in the bins around the block. That kept him away for a few nights, but he kept coming back and kept coming back until finally I snapped. I did the thing I told him I would not do. The police only move these people out, they never move them on but I could think of nothing else.

They came on a Sunday morning. I heard them enter, and listened to them through the door. They jerked him awake, asked his name and proof of his identity. He didn't have it. I heard him shuffling downstairs while the police made a call to the council – the landing and the stairwell were a stinking mess and needed a clean. They chapped on my door and told me he had gone. I thought that would be the end of it. It wasn't.

I registered a look of betrayal on his face.

"How can you do this, you know?" "I couldn't help it" I told him "You disturbed me."

"But you know I'm bad, right? I have nowhere to go, and outside it's dangerous and cold."

"Look.." He interrupted me, hushing me. He didn't want my voice to get too loud or other people would hear. When the police had found him on the stairs, they asked him where he came from. He told them Poland, although he'd told me earlier he was from Ukraine. I asked him why he'd changed this.

"You know, Ukraine is crazy, they might send me back there so I don't tell them, you know, that's thinking."

I took it in. When he told me, he was bad, he didn't just mean homeless. He had a drink problem. Along with having no documents, his situation was dire.

"I gonna leave here now for good" he said "I jus' come back to tell you this. I gonna have a cigarette here then I leave but don't call the police. Don't call the police."

I went into my flat and pondered what he had said. I couldn't really relate to him, I was just a stuck-up middle class boy. I also knew from the news, the homeless had a rough time of it, with metal studs being etched into outside benches and buildings to stop people sleeping on them.

But his presence almost literally on my doorstep, like the others before, had frightened me. As well as sleeping on that landing, they did the toilet on it. Also I had no real way of knowing whether they were benign or might break into my flat if they got comfortable enough.

Maybe I was just being paranoid, but I did what I thought was right at the time. I opened the curtains and looked over to the main street, bodies and the traffic blurring past quietly as I stood there at my window watching all go by.

Vallance Road

The road is being torn up
Down Vallance Road
Mechanised monsters

Digging holes and spewing concrete
Making way for a new Crossrail
The future is forever
Altering the face of the past

The youth of today
Chatter in parks
And on their iPhones

Police sirens sounding
Unheard amid the trees

There are no more bombs
No more rockets

The departed memories of history
Leaving their lessons unlearnt
Progress silences

Perverting ourselves
It is so easy
To lose
Through having gained

Depression is a Most Unwelcome Guest

I will confess I often get obsessed
With little things that taunt and bully me
Depression is a most unwelcome guest

It crawled in, bedded down and made a nest
That's built on guilt and self-disgust in me
I will confess I often get obsessed
With being weak and stupid, second-best

To all the world I see surrounding me
Depression is a most unwelcome guest
That lives inside my head and likes to jest
With words that sting, humiliating me

I will confess I often get obsessed
By angel's voices leaving me possessed
By echoing delusions, saddening me

Depression is a most unwelcome guest
That beats me down and gives my nerves unrest
And with this broken man I see reflecting me
I will confess I often get obsessed
Depression is a most unwelcome guest.

Losing My Mind on the Internet

Losing my mind on the Internet
Wasting my life in an endless daze
Getting a high that I can't forget

Floating away in an empty haze
Wasting my life in an endless daze
Pointlessly twittering thoughtless bunk
Floating away in an empty haze

Drifting online and I'm all but sunk
Pointlessly twittering pointless bunk
Boredom replacing reality
Drifting online and I'm all but sunk

Trapped in electric insanity
Boredom replacing reality
Chasing the shadows of friends unknown

Trapped in electric insanity
Music of madness that leaves me thrown
Chasing the shadows of friends unknown
Getting a high that I can't forget
Music of madness that leaves me thrown
Losing my mind on the Internet

I am a Sex and Love Addict

I am a sex and love addict
I live in a world of my own
I scour the internet for pretty prey
For burlesque dancers, chorus girls,
The ghosts of old loves past,

I yearn so desperately to love yet I get high
On sexual, romantic fantasy that is not real
I'm feeling really burdened by my terrible affliction
Will somebody please save me
From my sex and love addiction?
I am a sex and love addict
I live in the world of the city
I prowl the pubs and clubs for pretty prey
For working women, prostitutes

The ghosts of old loves past
I yearn so desperately to love
Yet I get high on one-night stands
That go nowhere and leave my soul in darkness
I'm feeling really burdened by my terrible affliction
Will somebody please save me
From my sex and love addiction?
We are sex and love addicts
Bound together in our sadness
Drowning in our sorrows, oppression and perversity
Joined in harmony

We appeal to a stronger, higher power
Oh, rescue us from ourselves!
We seek salvation - save our souls!
We're feeling really burdened by our terrible affliction
Will somebody please save us
From our sex and love addiction?

Conversations Are like Tennis Matches

Back-and-forth, back-and-forth
Back-and-forth, back-and-forth
You meet someone
Someone dressed like you

Who talks the same language
Spend a few minutes
Knocking some words around
Back-and-forth, back-and-forth
Back-and-forth, back-and-forth
Backhanders of wit

Forehands of great observation
Volleys of words that stun the listener
Back-and-forth, back-and-forth
Back-and-forth, back-and-forth

I tire very easily
It's always the other guy
Who has the last shot

Intimacy

She wants intimacy
She's into me, you see
We're on the same wavelength
We like the same things
She's there when I'm troubled
Or injured or hurt

And yet there's a wall
Between us as people
As she's after something
That I cannot give her
She wants intimacy
She's into me you see
She wants a physical love
Of a sexual kind

A romantic connection
For her peace of mind
Yet though I admire her
Respect and appreciate her
I cannot reciprocate her
I cannot sleep with her

Although she warms and she comforts me
In that sense, she just doesn't do it for me
I'm not trying to be nasty
But still I feel guilty
Even though it's useless

The feeling's so pointless
I'm not blind
I'm not gay
But there is no way
I can do it with her
It's not right, it's not fair
And I'm killing myself

With self-loathing and pity
Thinking and asking
"Why can't she be pretty?"
To me anyway

You might not think the same
That I'm playing a silly and self-centered game
You might be right
But I still stand firm

I'll only engage in that kind of action
With someone to whom I possess an attraction
And who fancies me back
But it's not her

I want to be friends
But it's hard to pretend
That's all she wants from me
She wants intimacy
She's into me, you see
But I'm not into her

The Dating Game

It's about what you want versus what you can get
What I want is a beautiful woman to love
I don't like going dating - it drives me insane
'Cos it's hard to relate to the women I see

What I want is a beautiful woman to love
But I can't seem to find the right lady for me
'Cos it's hard to relate to the women I see
And I can't be their boyfriend it just seems too hard
And I can't seem to find the right lady for me

For they're either too gorgeous for me to enjoy
And I can't be their boyfriend it just seems too hard
For they think I'm a geek and don't give me a glance
And they're either too gorgeous for me to enjoy
And I'm looking elsewhere for the things that I seek

For they think I'm a geek and don't give me a glance
And the girls I can have just don't do it for me
And I'm looking elsewhere for the things that I seek
It's frustrating to take the rejections I face

But the girls I can have just don't do it for me
Cos to me they are ugly or bonkers or dull
It's frustrating to take the rejections I face
But when I get a girl it just doesn't feel right
'Cos to me she is ugly or bonkers or dull

And I lose the desire for engaging with girls
So when I get a girl it just doesn't feel right
'Cos seducing or charming them feels so perverse
So I lose the desire for engaging with girls
I'm exhausted from trying to be what I'm not
'Cos seducing or charming them feels so perverse

And I'm turning them off with my low self esteem
I'm exhausted from trying to be what I'm not

Getting intimate feels so invasive at times
And I'm turning them off with my low self esteem
'Cos I'm moving too fast or I'm moving too slow
Getting intimate feels so invasive at times
When they want me too much or I want them too much

'Cos I'm moving too fast or I'm moving too slow
When connecting with women things soon hit a wall
When they want me too much or I want them too much
And the issue of sex keeps on rearing it's head

When connecting with women things soon hit a wall
'Cos I'm wanting some space and some time to myself
And the issue of sex keeps on rearing it's head
And I think "Am I gay 'cos I treat them this way?"
'Cos I'm wanting some time and some space to myself

I don't like to just flirt - it is sleazy and gross
And I think "Am I gay 'cos I'm feeling this way?"
But I know that I'm not for the need is still there
I don't like to just flirt - it is sleazy and gross

And I wonder at times if I'm better alone
But I know that I'm not for the need is still there
For the love and the company women provide
But I wonder at times if I'm better alone
But I'm not so I'll keep on pursuing my need

For the love and the company women provide
Life is hard and at times I believe I'm a fool
But I'm not so I'll keep on pursuing my need
Being friends with a woman can steady your soul

Life is hard and at times I believe I'm a fool
They distract me with laughter and lighten me up
Being friends with a woman can steady your soul
It is simple and fun and relaxing as well
They distract me with laughter and lighten me up

Not like dating, which seems a mysterious game
It is simple and fun and relaxing as well
And I find it more fun when there's no sex involved
Unlike dating which seems a mysterious game

Where you're cornered by life into making a choice
But I find life more fun when there's no sex involved
I don't like going dating it drives me insane
'Cos you're cornered by life into making a choice
That's about what you want versus what you can get.

When Polly Met Darren

When Polly met Darren, it seemed an ideal match
He was tall, proud and strong - he looked a perfect catch
Their first few dates went splendidly - the pair would talk for hours
He'd take her out to restaurants, and send her gifts and flowers
They bought a flat - it seemed their love would blossom and bear fruit
Until she found he really liked to scratch his athlete's foot

She asked "Why do you do it?" and he said "I can't explain
But when I feel the urge to scratch the itch I go insane"
"When I was very young, one time my feet were wet and sore
And my scratching nails said to the itch "OK, this time it's war"
"Since then I simply cannot stop, it really is a treat

To scratch my flaking, bleeding, battle-scarred and calloused feet"
Now Polly listened carefully, she heard what he was saying
And told him "Look it's fine. I'm really OK with your scratching"
"Take care not to go overboard and try to be discreet
Whatever time you feel the urge to scratch your itching feet"
She didn't mind at first but then it quickly became irritating
The scratching was relentless it was maddening and aggravating
At nights they were frequently coming to blows
She kept waking up to find him ravishing his toes
Then Polly finally had enough and threw a massive strop
Telling Darren "Please, my darling, all this scratching has to stop."
And Darren said "I will, my dear. My athlete's foot is history"
He then produced a ring and said "Oh Polly, will you marry me?"

The wedding was a great success with lots of cheer and laughter
The newlyweds ascended to their hotel wedding chamber
But as they entered Darren said "Dear wife, please wait a minute"
He sped away with unexpected haste into the toilet
As Polly listened at the door, she fell into despair
He was in the toilet making love to his feet and not to her!
Then Polly screamed "That's it! We're through! I'm getting a divorce!"
Her mind was made up then and there - she had no second thoughts
And Darren had to search again to find the perfect girl
To love, accept and understand him - itchy feet and all.

Breakup

"So that's what that feels like"
Reaching into the stale morning air
Envious rage oozing
From my eyes
Lying on the couch

My body suspended
In a silent tantrum
Mouthing your name

The night before
You had taken me to dinner
But it soon became apparent
Our relationship was finished
It had run its course

Your desire for me waning
Not surprised but disappointed
Because you needed someone
To look after you

And I was not that person
My manic affection
Having turned into
A grasping neediness

As I veered into depressing,
Anxious moods that you
Could neither comprehend
Nor cope with

I let you go without a struggle
Casting all remnants of you
Out of my life

Wiping your number off my phone
To stop myself stalking yo

What I think and feel
Is nothing to do with you now
But I stop short of feeling
Sorry for myself

When I remember
The broken hearts I've made
The tears I caused

And then I realize
"So that's what it feels like"

Karma Complex

The gods we worship,
The gods we fear,
Do not exist in some mythical place above

They exist among us
Fate is the invisible
Workings of our surroundings
Motivated by the rest
Of the living universe

Whose agenda may,
Or may not,
Conflict with our own
Conflict with mine
Karma,

If such a thing exists,
Is the way in which
Our actions
Rebound upon ourselves

Affecting our lives
It is this I fear,
This karma,

The forces of life
More powerful than me
Against whom I feel unable

To defend or justify myself
In any way
These forces seek to thwart
And punish me for my sins

My sins being weakness
Idling on benefits
Claiming mental illness

As an excuse to avoid responsibility
With distorted thinking giving me
Ideas above my capabilities
That can and must
Be slapped down by the forces

Exhausted paranoia
Soothed by the occasional bliss
Flowing and frothing
In a moment

Then ebbing away
As the fear of karma returns
Imagining the worst
To try and keep it at bay
Nothing is more humiliating

Than being complacent
Then being found out
Weaknesses and self-deceiving lies
Exposed
As the forces move in
To stamp me out

Learning Disability

The inability to learn
From one's mistakes
That is why we call it
A learning disability
In life

I have felt many things
I have felt fear
Of making mistakes
I have felt sorrow

For the state of the world
For those less fortunate
And ashamed
At my indifference to them

I have felt self-pity
At being weak
Unable to keep up
With the competitive world
Around me

Of not being the person
I feel I should be
In this
I have felt anger
When people

Have injured me
I have never forgiven them
Instead devoted myself
To hating them
Even when I could not
Outsmart or overpower them
Because to stop hating
Means to admit

That they were right
And I was wrong
So I kept hating
Throwing fists
That could always get
Thrown back with
Ten times the force
Reducing me to tantrums

The clenched fist
Unfolding to become
A slap to the face
Then another
And another
I go mad trying to win
The battles in my head
I never won in life
Hating myself
Screaming in protest

Trying to block out the liars
The enemies
The unwanted voices
Leading to self-denial
And total detachment

When I made a mistake
I never gained by it
But just pretended
It never happened
I never knew these people
I never heard those words
I never did those things
I never lived that life
Like I said, It's called a learning disability

The Ballad of Jack McGee

My name is Mr. Jack McGee
I'm a journalist by trade
The paper that I write for
Is very widely read

We've published many stories
Of a controversial slant
But the story that I have to tell
Is one we couldn't print

I was in Culver, years ago
Writing up a robbery
The locals had some stories
That intrigued and excited me

A camper said he'd seen a monster
Lurking by the river
The creature was of human shape
Only it was ten times bigger

The face was ugly, fierce and wild
It roared at him in anger
The camper fled in terror from it
Scared he was in danger
It wasn't the most plausible

Of stories that I've heard
But the man seemed reasonable and sane
I took him at his word
The camper showed me evidence
A huge footprint in the dirt
An abandoned car was lying close by

The shell was crushed and bent
I followed the road for half a mile
To a building in the hills
I saw a couple talking outside

Standing by the doors
The couple were two scientists
Elaine and David Banner
I asked them just a couple of questions,
Looking for an answer
But I all got was blank denial

Keeping me at bay
They tried their best to close me down
And make me go away
But I had a funny feeling
A reporter's intuition

I can tell when someone's lying
And concealing information
I waited 'til the time was right
Then snuck inside the building
I wanted to observe them
And see what they were doing

I got a little look inside
A cavernous laboratory
With graphs, charts and monitors
Everywhere before me
With all of it in disarray

The room looked such a mess
With upturned chairs and tables,
Splintered wood and broken glass
I ventured in, I heard a yell

Then someone grabbed my elbow
The two of them had seen me enter,
Watching from the shadows
David Banner gripped my arm
And threw me back outside

I knew then there was something
He was really keen to hide
I asked him straight up "What's the deal?"
He raised his arm and warned me
"Don't make me lose control.
You wouldn't like me when I'm angry."
I took the hint and backed away
Ready to retreat

And that was when the two of us
Were blasted off our feet
The science building was on fire
Flames were racing through it
And Banner scrambled to his feet
And rushed off back inside it

The flames were getting higher
And the heat was just unbearable
I stumbled off, looked back
And then I saw something...incredible
A ten-foot green-skinned creature
Walking through the flames
Growling, snarling furiously

The woman in his arms
I couldn't move from staring
At this truly awesome sight
The Hulk let out a roar and then
Raced off into the night

The girl was found a few hours later
Lying in the woods
There was no life left in her,
She had perished from her wounds

The cops interrogated me,
Checking out the matter
Of the death of both the woman
And her partner David Banner
He burnt to death inside the lab

As he came to her rescue
His body gone without a trace,
Lost in the inferno
The cops just shook their heads
When I informed them of the creature
It was the Hulk that caused the fire

This thing committed murder
It didn't matter who I told
No-one would believe it
But I knew the Hulk was real
And I was going to prove it

The Hulk just didn't disappear
He kept on turning up
As a mysterious and violent force
That nobody could stop
I tracked the Hulk across the land
Wherever someone saw it

I took a tranquiliser gun,
Hoping to subdue it
I chased the Hulk for many years
The more that I pursued him
The more I came to know his plight
The more I understood him

I was cornered one time
By a gangster with a knife
The Hulk showed up and took him down
The creature saved my life
I learned then that the creature

Was not completely evil
But more than that, I learned the Hulk
Was actually two people
A single man who walked the roads
And moved from place to place
Forced to hide the angry Hulk
Behind a human face

The Hulk was always on my mind
It maddened and it tortured me
I had to find the Hulk and trap him,
Learn his true identity

My grand obsession with this creature
Tore apart my marriage
To keep a loving home life going
Was more than I could manage
My colleagues all made fun of me
For following the Hulk

My editor thought I was nuts,
A total laughing stock
He told me "Kill this story, Jack,
It's totally ridiculous"
"You're throwing your career away.
Let it go - I'm serious."

I pinned my hopes upon the Hulk
To salvage my career
But there were times I got depressed
And fell into despair
But I stayed strong, I knew deep down
Just what I had to do

Determination drove me on
To see this story through
I was in the town of Wilmington
There'd been another sighting
My paper redirected me

Towards a nearby shooting
The town airport was under siege
Some terrorists had captured it
The army had the place surrounded
Hell-bent on retaking it
I took a chance, and quickly slipped
Behind the battle lines
Inside, some hostages were gathered,

Fearing for their lives Amid the sound of gunfire,
There was panic and confusion
As something unexpected happened
Causing a commotion

The Hulk emerged, as if from nowhere,
Crashing through a wall
His size, ferocity and power
Mesmerized them all

The terrorists made their retreat
And quickly fled the building
The Hulk gave chase and followed them,
Snarling and growling

A plane was waiting for the gang,
They all soon climbed aboard it
The Hulk just kept on running
As he made his way toward it

The plane rolled down the runway
As it's turbine engines flared
The savage grabbed a wing
As it took off into the air

A gunman fired upon the Hulk,
Some bullets hit the engine
The Hulk was thrown into the sky
Caught up in the explosion
He landed hard upon the ground
The impact made a crater

I made my way to find
The stricken body of the creature
The Hulk lay there completely still
And then began to change
Reverting to his human form
I recognized his face
A man I long believed was dead

The scientist David Banner
The realization dawned on me
With sadness and with horror
His flickering eyes snapped open
He looked up and said to me

"The Hulk is finally destroyed
It's finished now - I'm free"
The Army gathered round
And carried Banner's corpse away

I stood back, completely stunned
Not knowing what to say
I got back to my office
And I found a message for me
An order from the government
To never print my story

I punched the wall in anger
This was simply too upsetting
All my pursuits and all my struggles
All of it - for nothing!
I settled down eventually
Coming to my senses

I didn't want to risk my job
I knew the consequences
I wondered home alone that night
Whistling in the dark
And shed a tear in memory
Of the man they called the Hulk.

Love Is

A feeling
An invisible
But very real feeling
A feeling between people
A strong feeling
A feeling of caring
A feeling of desire
Love is you
Love is me
Love is what binds us
Together in society

Love is emotional
Love is physical
Love is paternal
Love is familial
Love is platonic
Sometimes love is sexual

Love is not loneliness
Love is not jealousy
Love is not greed
Love is respect
Love is not absolute
Love is not binding
Love is not possession
Love is not stalking
Love is not obsession
Love is not living in fear of rejection

Love is not a fairytale
Love is not a fantasy
Love is not voyeurism
Love is not pornography
Love is neither hate nor worship of another
Love is acceptance
Love is compromising

Love is empathising
Love is understanding
Love is listening
Love is sympathetic
But sympathy should never be
A substitute for love

Love is not gaining
Love is giving
Love is sharing
Love is not violence
Love is not abuse
Love is not rape
Love is not perversion
Love is never harm

Love is not guilt
Love is not excuses
Love is not dishonesty
Love is openness
Love is not easy
Love is not leisurely
Love needs work
Love is hard

Love is a risk
Love is dangerous
Love is transformation
Love is change

Love is not the future
Love is not the past
Love is the present
Love is in the moment

Love is not permanent
Love is not holding on
Sometimes love is

Letting go and moving on
Love is in everyone
Every living being
That interacts

With the environment
To live without love
Is to never live at all
We all laugh
We all cry
We all live
We all die
But those who really live
Love

Falling Forward

When we are young
Some of us say
"When I grow up I want to be an actor
I want to be a writer
I want to be a singer
I want to be a painter
I want to be a film-maker
I want to inspire
I want to create

I want to be an artist"
But others say
"That's all well and good
But you need something
To fall back on"

So fall back
Fall back on your education
Fall back on your job
Fall back on the sympathy
Of all your friends and family

Fall back on charity
Fall back into poverty
Fall back on the dole

Fall back on the insecurity
Eating away at your soul
Fall back on hesitation
Fall back on procrastination
Fall back on frustration

Fall back on never working hard enough
Fall back on the fact

That you are just not good enough
Fall back on misery
Fall back on mediocrity

Fall back on disillusion
Fall back on confusion
About who you really are
Fall back on wild, lazy notions
About being a superstar

Fall back on the truth
That being an artist
Is not about being famous
It's about finding
And creating work
For yourself and other artists

There's this modern myth
About being an artist
It's that either you are famous
Or you are nothing

That unless you're a celebrity
You don't count for anything
It's a misleading nonsense
A fallacy and distortion
This is the truth
Of a real artist's situation
It's not the fame
But the process
Of artistic creation
That's the real reason
We do what we do
This the way in which
We connect with the world around us

This is how we live
Through our art
So if you're prepared
To accept this reality
If you want it that much
If this really is your destiny
Don't fall back
Fall forward

Fall forward on your passion
Fall forward on ambition
Fall forward, embrace
Your artistic condition

Fall forward to stay alive
Fall forward on anything
It takes to survive
Fall forward on your failures
As well as your successes
Fall forward on your own terms
And no-one else's

Fall forward on your face
Fall forward on embarrassment
Fall forward in disgrace

Because if you try to avoid failure
You going to fail
Try to avoid disappointment
You are going to be disappointed
Failure and disappointment
Affect all of us
No matter what choices we make
In this life
If you haven't suffered
You will

So you can either suffer
Or screw yourself up

Through being too afraid to suffer
The only way to move forward
Is not to fall back
But to fall forward
And keep on rising
Keep on rising
Keep on learning
Keep on falling forward

This Is Who I Am

My name is Alain English
I come from Aberdeen

The darkest and the strangest
Scottish poet ever seen

Growing up in Aberdeen
It felt a little foolish

To have a Scottish accent
With a name like Alain English

I grew up disadvantaged
In a vulnerable position

I have a disability
An autistic condition

In my head I felt alive
Like I could be a hero

In real life things were different
My social skills were zero

I tried to hide it acting hard
Instead I looked a fool

And brought myself humiliation
Shame and ridicule

The bullying that I deserved
Would send me home in tears

To this day I still can hear
Their laughter in my ears

The lovely girls I knew at school
Would make me happy dreaming

But when I tried to make a move
The girls would run off screaming

I can't say that I blame them
I'm a voyeur and a freak

I'm stupid and self-centered
I'm childish and I'm weak

But I possess a power inside
For poetry sublime

For verbal pyrotechnics
And dark, disturbing rhyme

I can show you other worlds
Both terrible and magical

Be romantic and hilarious
Provocative and political

You can take me, you can leave me
I don't give a damn

This is my identity
This is who I am